WHO WOULD WIN?®

BLUE WHALE

VS.

MOSQUITO

BY
JERRY PALLOTTA

ILLUSTRATED BY
ROB BOLSTER

Scholastic Inc.

The publisher would like to thank the following for their
kind permission to use their photographs in this book:
Photos ©: 4: MR1805/Getty Images; 5: arlindo71/Getty Images; 13: Young Swee Ming/
Shutterstock; 18: Roberto Machado Noa/Shutterstock; 20 galaxy: ESA/Hubble & NASA, M
Gullieuszik and the GASP team; 24: Jian Fan/Getty Images; 25: Shonyjade/Shutterstock

To my two new grand mosquitoes, Guy and Trent. Also a big thank-you to Boston Children's Hos;
—J.P.

Thank you to the United States Coast Guard for their heroic work.
—R.B.

Text copyright © 2024 by Jerry Pallotta.
Illustrations copyright © 2024 by Rob Bolster.

Library of Congress Cataloging-in-Publication Data available
ISBN 978-1-339-00094-7

10 9 8 7 6 5 4 3 2 1   24 25 26 27 28

Printed in the U.S.A.   40
First printing, 2024

What if a blue whale came to the surface of the ocean and swam next to a mosquito? It could happen! Blue whale versus mosquito! If they could fight, who do you think would win?

MEET THE BLUE WHALE

Scientific name: *Balaenoptera musculus*

The blue whale is the largest animal that has ever lived on Earth. It is bigger than the biggest dinosaurs. The blue whale is even larger than the megalodon, an extinc giant shark.

DEFINITION
To be extinct means to no longer be a living animal species.

MAMMAL FACT
The blue whale is a sea mammal. It lives in the ocean. Blue whales never walk on land!

MEET THE MOSQUITO

Scientific name: *Culicidae*

The mosquito is an insect. It is one creature that no one likes. That's because mosquitoes bite many animals, including humans. They drill into flesh and suck blood.

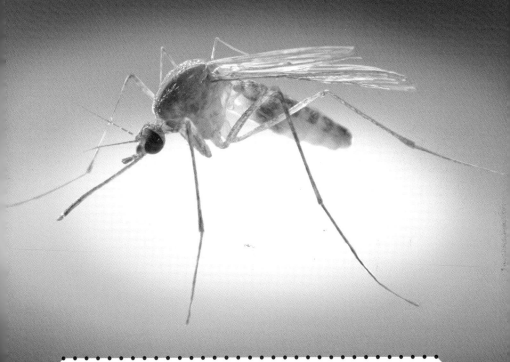

MOSQUITO LOVE
Maybe bats like mosquitoes because they eat them.

DID YOU KNOW?
Only female mosquitoes bite animals.

WORLDWIDE

Blue whales live in every ocean except the Arctic Ocean. You might see one in the water near Baja California, Iceland, Hawaii, or the Azores.

When taking care of their young, blue whales swim to the warmer waters near the equator.

Ar

Iceland

North America

Hawaii

Azores Islands

Baja California

Pacific Ocean

Atlantic Ocean

— — — — — — — — — — equator —

South America

OLD AGE FACT
A blue whale could live 90 years. Humans can live to be over 100.

Antarctic Ocean

WARM AREAS

Mosquitoes live in warm areas all over the world.
Mosquitoes cannot survive in the cold.

> **YOUNG AGE FACT**
> *Mosquitoes usually live
> less than two months.*

ean

urope

Asia

ica

**Indian
Ocean**

**Pacific
Ocean**

Australia

> **COLD FACT**
> *There are no
> mosquitoes in Antarctica.*

Antarctica

PARTS OF A BLUE WHALE

tail

FACT
A blue whale does not have teeth. Sorry, dentists!

DID YOU KNOW?
A blue whale's length is about 400 Who Would Win? books side by side.

body

blowhole

pectoral fin

head

eye

baleen

SIZE FACT
A blue whale's tongue is as heavy as an elephant.

tongue

PARTS OF A MOSQUITO

A mosquito is made of three main parts: head, thorax, abdomen.

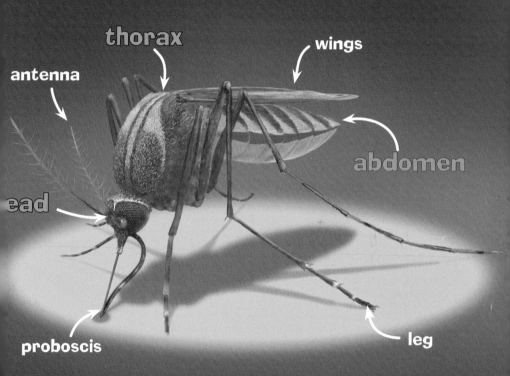

thorax

wings

antenna

abdomen

head

proboscis

leg

BIGGER

Is any living thing bigger than a blue whale?
The giant sequoia tree is bigger. The largest
giant sequoia tree in the world is called the
General Sherman Tree. It is in California.
Its trunk is 36 feet thick at the base.

COMPARE

scale
100 feet

whale shark

megalodon

blue whale

Giganotosaurus

human

SMALLER

What is smaller than a mosquito? The smallest known insect is the fairyfly. Fairyflies are found throughout the world.

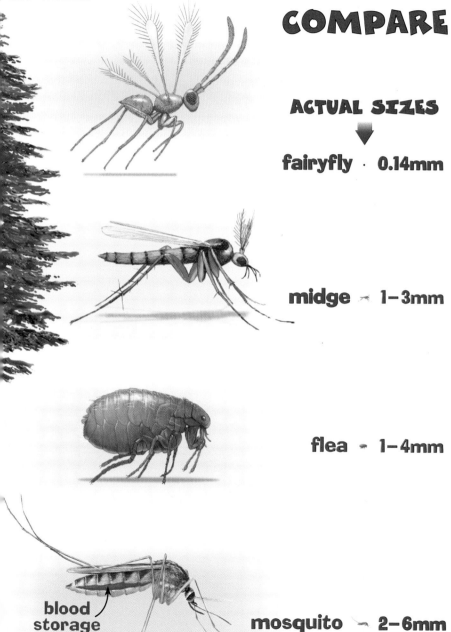

COMPARE

ACTUAL SIZES

fairyfly · 0.14mm

midge ~ 1–3mm

flea · 1–4mm

blood storage

mosquito ~ 2–6mm

BLUE WHALE FACE

This is what a blue whale's face looks like.

Blue whales have bluish-gray skin with 80–100 deep grooves along the length of their bodies. Every blue whale's groove pattern is unique!

MOSQUITO FACE

This is what a mosquito's face looks like. Yikes!

Mosquitoes have two eyes. They also have two antennae. The antennae help them detect sounds around them.

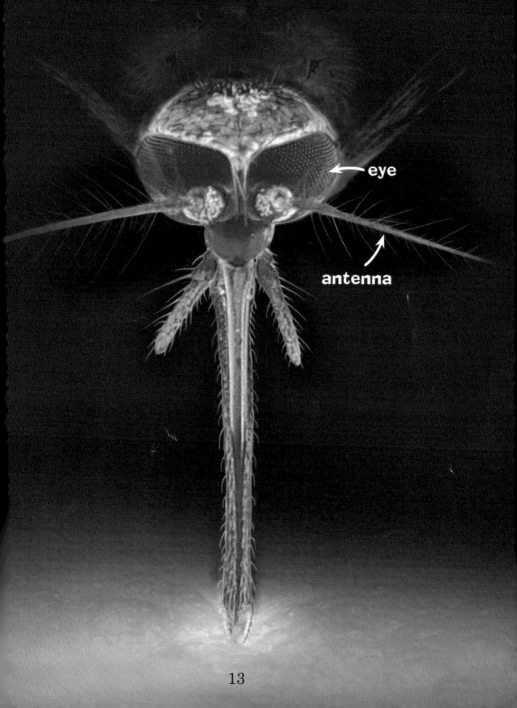

eye

antenna

FINS

This is what blue whale fins look like. The blue whale ha
one pectoral fin on each side to help it swim and a small
dorsal fin on its back.

pectoral fins } top view

dorsal fin   side view

RESEARCH
*What is the difference between
pectoral fins and dorsal fins?*

SPEED
*Blue whales can swim
up to 25 miles per hour.*

WINGS

This is what mosquito wings look like. Mosquitoes can beat their wings up to 500 times per second.

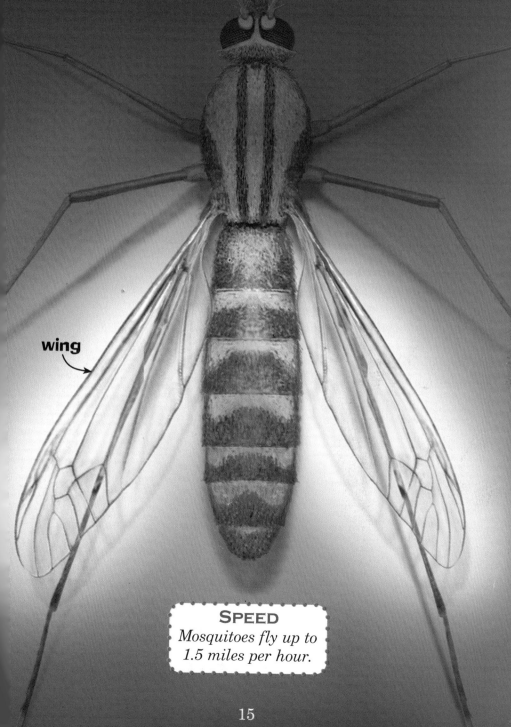

wing

SPEED
Mosquitoes fly up to 1.5 miles per hour.

BLUE WHALE TAIL

A blue whale tail is also called its fluke. It can be 15 feet across. People love to watch whales dive. You get a great look at their flukes!

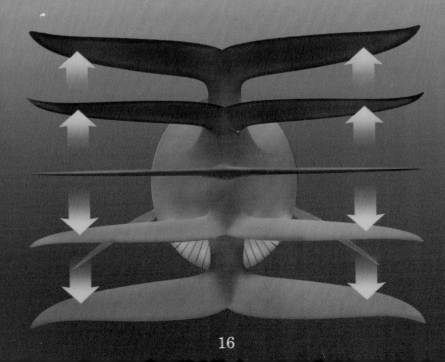

GROUP FACT
A group of whales is called a pod.

SOLO FACT
Blue whales usually live alone.

JUMP FACT
When a whale jumps out of the water, it is breaching. A blue whale rarely breaches.

SWARM

When there is a large group of mosquitoes, it is called a swarm of mosquitoes. No one wants to get caught in a swarm of mosquitoes.

FOOD FACT
Dragonflies eat mosquitoes.

PREY FACT
Spiders, bats, birds, and toads also eat mosquitoes.

BLUE WHALE HEART

A blue whale heart is as large as a small car.

BLUE WHALE HEART

BEAT FACT
A blue whale heart beats only once every ten seconds.

SIZE FACT
A blue whale heart weighs about 1,000 pounds.

MOSQUITO HEART

To see a mosquito heart, you would need a microscope.

MOSQUITO HEART

STETHOSCOPE

When a doctor or nurse listens to your heart or your lungs, they use a stethoscope. A stethoscope amplifies body sounds.

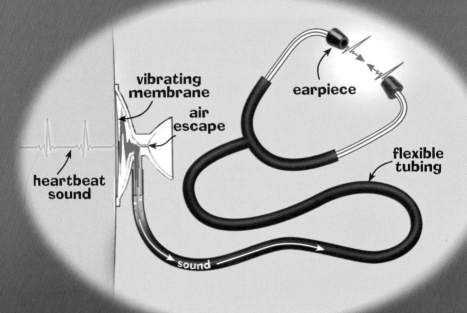

vibrating membrane

earpiece

air escape

flexible tubing

heartbeat sound

sound

TELESCOPE

A telescope allows you to look at things far away. What you've always thought was a star could be a galaxy!

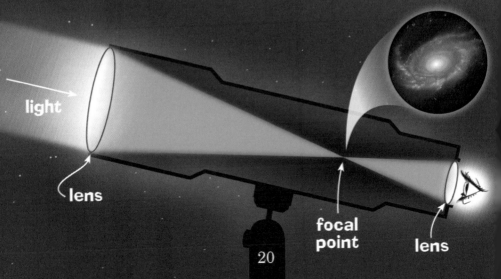

light

lens

focal point

lens

PERISCOPE

A periscope is a device that allows you to look around corners or obstacles. Submarines have periscopes.

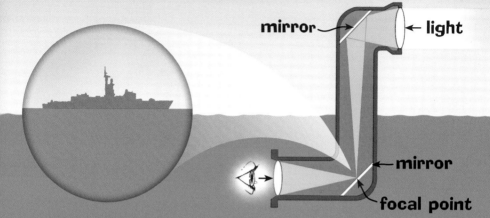

mirror — light

mirror

focal point

MICROSCOPE

A microscope is a device with a lens that visually enlarges tiny images. It allows scientists to see little things, like the hairs on a mosquito's leg. A regular microscope cannot see a virus because a virus is too small. A virus can be seen with an electron microscope, which can magnify even smaller things.

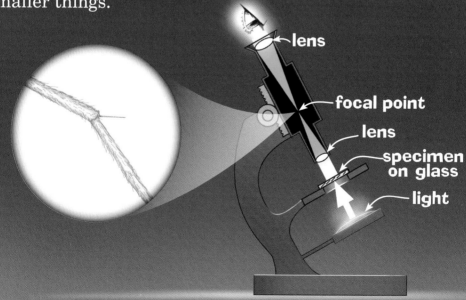

lens

focal point

lens

specimen on glass

light

HOW?

Think! How could a tiny mosquito hurt a giant blue whale? It couldn't punch it. It couldn't kick it. Mosquitoes don't have teeth.

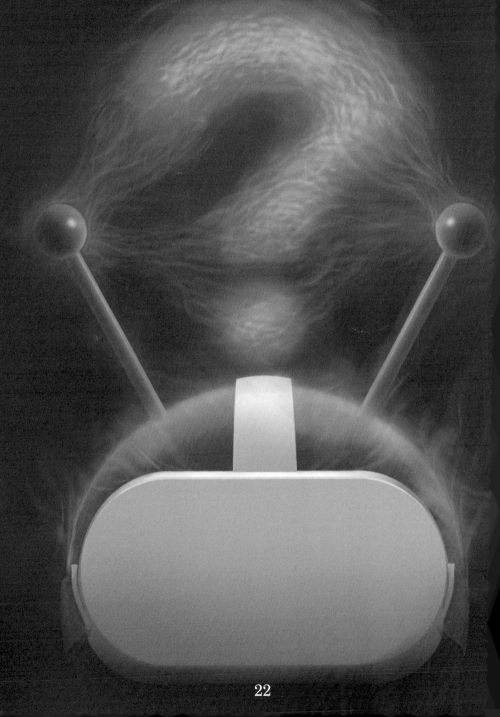

DISEASE

It might be far-fetched, but there is a way. Mosquitoes have a unique weapon. The mosquito could be carrying a dangerous disease and inject it into the whale.

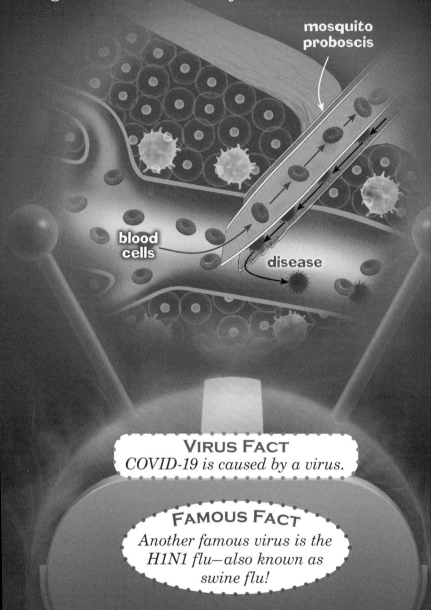

mosquito proboscis

blood cells

disease

VIRUS FACT
COVID-19 is caused by a virus.

FAMOUS FACT
Another famous virus is the H1N1 flu—also known as swine flu!

The diseases mosquitoes might carry have scary names like malaria, dengue fever, Zika virus, West Nile virus, and chikungunya virus.

CELL

This is what a cell looks like. The cell is the basic unit of life. It's what all life is made of.

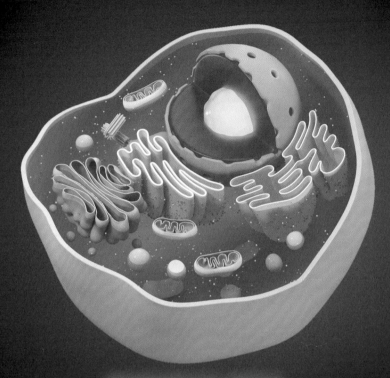

HUMAN CELL

The human body has about 37 trillion cells in it. There are blood cells, muscle cells, bone cells, skin cells, brain cells, and more. This is what 37 trillion looks like:

37,000,000,000,000.

That's a lot of cells!

DID YOU KNOW?
Animals and plants are also made of cells.

VIRUS

Every human body has viruses in it. This is what some viruses look like. You can see them only with the help of a powerful electron microscope.

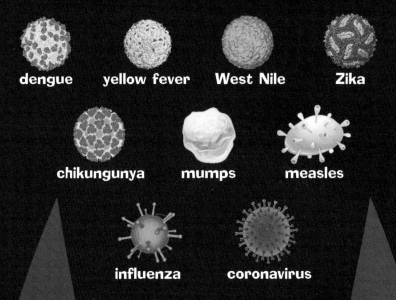

dengue   yellow fever   West Nile   Zika

chikungunya   mumps   measles

influenza   coronavirus

Good viruses help you digest food. Bad viruses make you sick.

OUTER SPACE THOUGHT

If aliens came to Earth, they might see each one of us as trillions of cells and millions of viruses rather than as single beings.

INVADERS

A virus cannot live on its own or multiply on its own. It has to invade a healthy cell to survive.

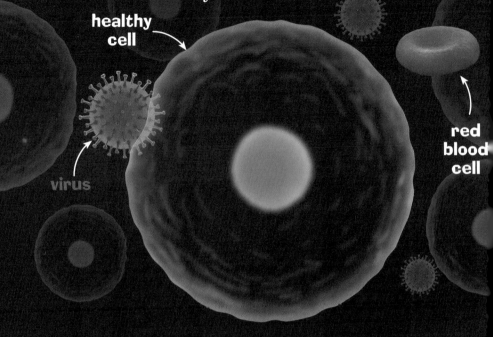

healthy cell

virus

red blood cell

Uh-oh! The virus is now in a cell. This is how you get colds, flu, fevers, and other sicknesses.

infected cell

MEDICINE

When a virus makes you sick, your body starts to fight it! Some cells in your body, called white blood cells, find the virus and attack it.

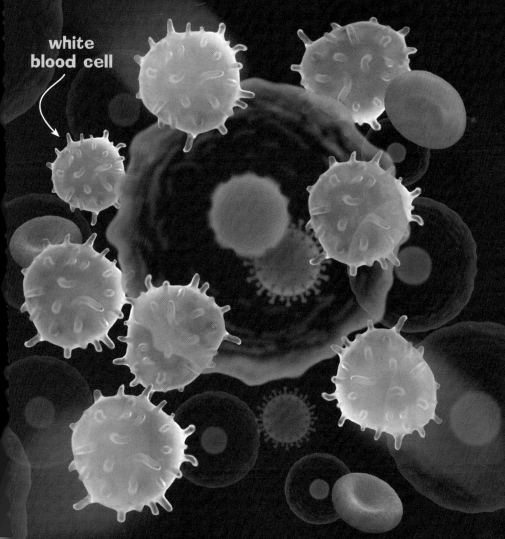

white blood cell

When you're sick, you should get lots of rest and drink water to help your body fight the infection.

Here is the question: Can a virus attack a whale? Can a virus weaken a blue whale, the largest animal that ever lived on Earth?

A strong wind blows a swarm of mosquitoes off the coast and over the ocean.

A blue whale is swimming nearby, feeding on krill.

The blue whale slaps its tail and immediately wipes out hundreds of the mosquitoes.

The mosquitoes fall to the surface of the ocean and small fish eat them for dinner.

I guess we could say the blue whale wins. It killed hundreds of mosquitoes.

The blue whale dives under the water and keeps swimming. Some of the mosquitoes that are left wait for the whale to surface. A few of the mosquitoes bit the whale before it went underwater, but its skin and blubber are so thick that the whale didn't notice.

The whale surfaces and opens its mouth to feed on krill.

A sneaky mosquito enters the mouth of the whale and bites a soft spot on its tongue. Uh-oh! This is a different story. The mosquito is carrying a virus.

Another mosquito bites the whale on its gums. Both mosquitoes inject the blue whale with a virus.

The blue whale does not die. It gets really sick and feels awful for two weeks. It's no fun being sick. Who would you say won this battle?

WHO HAS THE ADVANTAGE? CHECKLIST

BLUE WHALE		MOSQUITO
☐	Size	☐
☐	Speed	☐
☐	Eyesight	☐

If you were the author, how would you write the ending?